W9-AAT-418

Happy
Valentines
Day ob

Bobby
& Stan

AFFIRMATIONS

itty**bitty**books™

AFFIRMATIONS

THOMAS NELSON PUBLISHERS
Nashville

Published in Nashville, Tennessee by Thomas Nelson, Publishers and distributed in Canada by Lawson Falle, Ltd., Cambridge, Ontario.

**Library of Congress
Cataloging-in-Publication Data**

Bible. English. New King James.
    Selections. Affirmations.
        p.   cm. — (An Itty Bitty book)
    ISBN 0-8407-6852-4
    I. Title. II. Series.
BS391.2.B3643 1992
220.5′2036—dc20   92-29039
                                          CIP

Printed in Singapore.
1 2 3 4 5 6 7 — 98 97 96 95 94 93

Contents

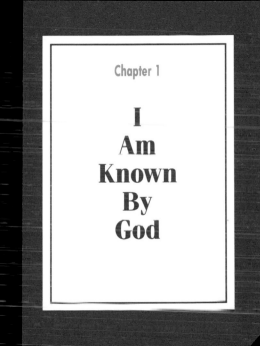

Chapter 1

I
Am
Known
By
God

O Lord, You have searched me and known me. You know my sitting down and my rising up; You understand my thought afar off. You comprehend my path and my lying down, And are acquainted with all my ways.

Psalm 139:1–3

Every way of a man is right in his own eyes, But the Lord weighs the hearts.

Proverbs 21:2

My frame was not hidden from You, When I was made in secret, And skillfully wrought in the lowest parts of the earth. Your eyes saw my substance, being yet unformed. And in Your book they all were written, The days fashioned for me.

Psalm 139:15–16

The spirit of a man is the lamp of the Lord, Searching all the inner depths of his heart.

Proverbs 20:27

For the Lord does not see as man sees; for man looks at the outward appearance, but the Lord looks at the heart.

1 Samuel 16:7

But He knows the way that I take;
When He has tested me, I shall come
forth as gold.

Job 23:10

Search me, O God, and know my
heart; Try me, and know my anxieties;
And see if there is any wicked way in
me, And lead me in the way everlasting.

Psalm 139:23-24

Are not two sparrows sold for a copper coin? And not one of them falls to the ground apart from your Father's will. But the very hairs of your head are all numbered. Do not fear therefore; you are of more value than many sparrows."

Matthew 10:29-31

The eyes of the Lord are on the righteous, And His ears are open to their cry. The righteous cry out, and the Lord hears, And delivers them out of all their troubles.

Psalm 34:15, 17

The Lord is good, A stronghold in the day of trouble; And He knows those who trust in Him.

Nahum 1:7

And when you pray, do not use vain repetitions as the heathen do. For they think that they will be heard for their many words. Therefore do not be like them. For your Father knows the things you have need of before you ask Him."

Matthew 6:7-8

And do not seek what you should eat or what you should drink, nor have an anxious mind.

"For all these things the nations of the world seek after, and your Father knows that you need these things. But seek the kingdom of God, and all these things shall be added to you."

Luke 12:29-31

Nevertheless the solid foundation of God stands, having this seal: "The Lord knows those who are His," and, "Let everyone who names the name of Christ depart from iniquity."

2 Timothy 2:19

or the ways of man are before the eyes of the Lord, And He ponders all his paths.

Proverbs 5:21

And by this we know that we are of the truth, and shall assure our hearts before Him.

For if our heart condemns us, God is greater than our heart, and knows all things.

1 John 3:19-20

And He said to them, "You are those who justify yourselves before men, but God knows your hearts. For what is highly esteemed among men is an abomination in the sight of God."

Luke 16:15

So we may boldly say, "The Lord is my helper, I will not fear. What can man do to me?"

Hebrews 13:6

So God, who knows the heart, acknowledged them, by giving them the Holy Spirit just as He did to us, And made no distinction between us and them, purifying their hearts by faith."

Acts 15:8-9

And he believed in the Lord, and He accounted it to him for righteousness.

Genesis 15:6

I, even I, am He who comforts you. Who are you that you should be afraid of a man who will die, and of a son of man who will be made like grass?"

Isaiah 51:12

Moreover whom He predestined, these He also called; whom He called, these He also justified; and whom He justified, these He also glorified.

Romans 8:30

When my spirit was overwhelmed within me, Then You knew my path. In the way in which I walk. . . . I cried out to You, O Lord: I said, "You are my refuge."

Psalm 142:3, 5

My soul, wait silently for God alone, for my expectation is from Him.

Psalm 62:5

Then hear from heaven Your dwelling place, and forgive, and give to everyone according to all his ways, whose heart You know (for You alone know the hearts of the sons of men)."

2 Chronicles 6:30

But know that the Lord has set apart for Himself him who is godly; the Lord will hear when I call to Him.

Psalm 4:3

Lift up your eyes on high, and see who has created these things, Who brings out their host by number; He calls them all by name, by the greatness of His might and the strength of His power; not one is missing.

Isaiah 40:26

The Lord is my shepherd; I shall not want.

Psalm 23:1

If any of you lacks wisdom, let him ask of God, who gives to all liberally and without reproach, and it will be given to him.

James 1:5

Being confident of this very thing, that He who has begun a good work in you will complete it until the day of Jesus Christ.

Philippians 1:6

For the Lord God is a sun and shield; the Lord will give grace and glory; no good thing will He withhold from those who walk uprightly.

Psalm 84:11

Your ears shall hear a word behind you, saying, "This is the way, walk in it," whenever you turn to the right hand or whenever you turn to the left.

Isaiah 30:21

Then I will give them a heart to know Me, that I am the Lord; and they shall be my people, and I will be their God, for they shall return to Me with their whole heart."

Jeremiah 24:7

Chapter 2

I
Am
Loved
By
God

But I am poor and needy; Yet the Lord thinks upon me. You are my help and my deliverer.

Psalm 40:17

The Lord your God in your midst, The Mighty One, will save; He will rejoice over you with gladness, He will quiet you in His love, He will rejoice over you with singing."

Zephaniah 3:17

But because the Lord loves you, and because He would keep the oath which He swore to your fathers, the Lord has brought you out with a mighty hand.

Deuteronomy 7:8

Therefore humble yourselves under the mighty hand of God, that He may exalt you in due time, casting all your care upon Him, for He cares for you.

1 Peter 5:6-7

Let us love one another, for love is of God; and everyone who loves is born of God and knows God. He who does not love does not know God, for God is love. In this the love of God was manifested toward us, that God has sent His only begotten Son into the world, that we might live through Him.

1 John 4:7-9

I in them, and You in Me; that they may be made perfect in one, and that the world may know that You have sent Me, and have loved them as You have loved Me."

John 17:23

But God demonstrates His own love toward us, in that while we were still sinners, Christ died for us.

Romans 5:8

I am persuaded that neither death nor life, nor angels nor principalities nor powers, nor things present nor things to come, nor height nor depth, nor any other created thing, shall be able to separate us from the love of God which is in Christ Jesus our Lord.

Romans 8:38–39

But when the kindness and the love of God our Savior toward man appeared, not by works of righteousness which we have done, but according to His mercy He saved us, through the washing of regeneration and renewing of the Holy Spirit.

Titus 3:4–5

God, who is rich in mercy, because of His great love with which He loved us, even when we were dead in trespasses, made us alive together with Christ.

Ephesians 2:4–5

The Lord your God turned the curse into a blessing for you, because the Lord your God loves you.

Deuteronomy 23:5

Jesus knew that His hour had come that He should depart from this world to the Father, having loved His own who were in the world, He loved them to the end.

John 13:1

By this we know love, because He laid down His life for us.

1 John 3:16

For God so loved the world that He gave His only begotten Son, that whoever believes in Him should not perish but have everlasting life."

John 3:16

You will keep him in perfect peace, whose mind is stayed on You, because he trusts in You.

Isaiah 26:3

Now therefore, if you will indeed obey
My voice and keep My covenant, then
you shall be a special treasure to Me
above all people; for all the earth
is Mine."

Exodus 19:5

If I say, "My foot slips," your mercy,
O Lord, will hold me up.

Psalm 94:18

The hand of our God is upon all those for good who seek Him, but His power and His wrath are against all those who forsake Him."

Ezra 8:22

Let us hold fast the confession of our hope without wavering, for He who promised is faithful.

Hebrews 10:23

For the Lord loves justice, and
does not forsake His saints; they are
preserved forever, but the descendants
of the wicked shall be cut off.

Psalm 37:28

I will be a Father to you, and you shall
be My sons and daughters, says the
Lord Almighty."

2 Corinthians 6:18

He will guard the feet of His saints, but the wicked shall be silent in darkness. For by strength no man shall prevail."

1 Samuel 2:9

If they obey and serve Him, they shall spend their days in prosperity, and their years in pleasures.

Job 36:11

In this is love, not that we loved God, but that He loved us and sent His Son to be the propitiation for our sins. We love HIm because He first loved us.

1 John 4:10, 19

The Father Himself loves you, because you have loved Me, and have believed that I came forth from God."

John 16:27

He who has My commandments and keeps them, it is he who loves Me. And he who loves Me will be loved by My Father, and I will love him and manifest Myself to him."

John 14:21

Behold what manner of love the Father has bestowed on us, that we should be called children of God!

1 John 3:1

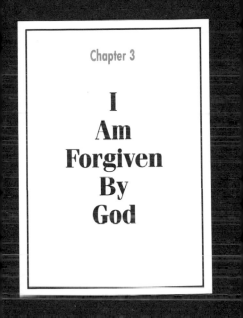

Chapter 3

I Am Forgiven By God

Come now, and let us reason together," Says the Lord, "Though your sins are like scarlet, They shall be as white as snow; Though they are red like crimson, They shall be as wool."

Isaiah 1:18

But let each one examine his own work, and then he will have rejoicing in himself alone, and not in another.

Galatians 6:4

The Spirit Himself bears witness with our spirit that we are children of God, and if children, then heirs—heirs of God and joint heirs with Christ, if indeed we suffer with Him, that we may also be glorified together.

Romans 8:16-17

In Him we have redemption through His blood, the forgiveness of sins, according to the riches of His grace.

Ephesians 1:7

He will again have compassion on us, And will subdue our iniquities. You will cast all our sins Into the depths of the sea.

Micah 7:19

For I will be merciful to their unrighteousness, and their sins and their lawless deeds I will remember no more."

Hebrews 8:12

Bless the Lord, O my soul, And forget not all His benefits: Who forgives all your iniquities, Who heals all your diseases, Who redeems your life from destruction.

Psalm 103:2-4

Return to the Lord your God, For He is gracious and merciful, Slow to anger, and of great kindness; And He relents from doing harm.

Joel 2:13

And the prayer of faith will save the sick, and the Lord will raise him up. And if he has committed sins, he will be forgiven.

James 5:15

If we say that we have no sin, we deceive ourselves, and the truth is not in us. If we confess our sins, He is faithful and just to forgive us our sins and to cleanse us from all unrighteousness.

1 John 1:8-9

Sing praise to the Lord, you saints of His, And give thanks at the remembrance of His holy name. For His anger is but for a moment, His favor is for life; Weeping may endure for a night, But joy comes in the morning.

Psalm 30:4–5

Blessed is he whose transgression is forgiven, Whose sin is covered. Blessed is the man to whom the Lord does not impute iniquity, And in whose spirit there is no guile. . . . I said, "I will confess my transgressions to the Lord," And You forgave the iniquity of my sin.

Psalm 32:1-2, 5

I will cleanse them from all their iniquity by which they have sinned against Me, and I will pardon all their iniquities by which they have sinned and by which they have transgressed against Me.

Jeremiah 33:8

If we say that we have no sin, we deceive ourselves, and the truth is not in us. If we confess our sins, He is faithful and just to forgive us our sins and to cleanse us from all unrighteousness.

1 John 1:8-9

He has delivered us from the power of darkness and translated us into the kingdom of the Son of His love, in whom we have redemption through His blood, the forgiveness of sins.

Colossians 1:13-14

I, even I, am He who blots out your transgressions for My own sake; And I will not remember your sins."

Isaiah 43:25

I have blotted out, like a thick cloud,
your transgressions, and like a cloud,
your sins. Return to Me, for I
have redeemed you."

Isaiah 44:22

But I have prayed for you, that your
faith should not fail; and when you have
returned to Me, strengthen your
brethren."

Luke 22:32

Then they cried out to the Lord in their trouble, And He saved them out of their distresses. He brought them out of darkness and the shadow of death, And broke their chains in pieces.

Psalm 107:13-14

But when the wicked turns from his wickedness and does what is lawful and right, he shall live because of it."

Ezekiel 33:19

But He was wounded for our transgressions, He was bruised for our iniquities; The chastisement for our peace was upon Him, And by His stripes we are healed.

Isaiah 53:5

I, even I, am He who blots out your transgressions for My own sake; and I will not remember your sins."

Isaiah 43:25

Now may the God of peace Himself sanctify you completely; and may your whole spirit, soul, and body be preserved blameless at the coming of our Lord Jesus Christ.

1 Thessalonians 5:23

For sin shall not have dominion over you, for you are not under law but under grace.

Romans 6:14

For the grace of God that brings
salvation has appeared to all men,
teaching us that, denying ungodliness
and wordly lusts, we should live soberly,
righteously, and godly in the present
age, looking for the blessed hope and
glorious appearing of our great God and
Savior Jesus Christ.

Titus 2:11-13

The Lord is not slack concerning His promise, as some count slackness, but is longsuffering toward us, not willing that any should perish but that all should come to repentance.

2 Peter 3:9

And it shall come to pass that whoever calls on the name of the Lord shall be saved."

Acts 2:21

So you shall serve the Lord your God, and He will bless your bread and your water. And I will take sickness away from the midst of you."

Exodus 23:25

For I will be merciful to their unrighteousness, and their sins and their lawless deeds I will remember no more."

Hebrews 8:12

Then He adds, "Their sins and their lawless deeds I will remember no more. Now where there is remission of these, there is no longer an offering for sin."

Hebrews 10:17-18

It is good that you grasp this, and also not remove your hand from the other; for he who fears God will escape them all.

Ecclesiastes 7:18

Chapter 4

I
Am
Affirmed
By
God

He delivered me from my strong enemy, From those who hated me, For they were too strong for me. They confronted me in the day of my calamity, But the Lord was my support. He also brought me out into a broad place; He delivered me because He delighted in me.

Psalm 18:17–19

Now may the God of peace Himself sanctify you completely; and may your whole spirit, soul, and body be preserved blameless at the coming of our Lord Jesus Christ.

1 Thessalonians 5:23

He who gets wisdom loves his own soul; He who keeps understanding will find good.

Proverbs 19:8

Give attention to my words; Incline your ear to my sayings. Do not let them depart from your eyes; Keep them in the midst of your heart; For they are life to those who find them, And health to all their flesh. Keep your heart with all diligence, For out of it spring the issues of life.

Proverbs 4:20–23

I will bring the blind by a way they did not know; I will lead them in paths they have not known. I will make darkness light before them, And crooked places straight. These things I will do for them, And not forsake them.

Isaiah 42:16

You will light my lamp; The Lord my God will enlighten my darkness.

Psalm 18:28

Trust in the Lord with all your heart, And lean not to your own understanding; In all your ways acknowledge Him, And He shall direct your paths.

Proverbs 3:5-6

Hope deferred makes the heart sick, But when the desire comes, it is a tree of life.

Proverbs 13:12

Coming to Him as to a living stone, rejected indeed by men, but chosen by God and precious, you also, as living stones, are being built up a spiritual house, a holy priesthood, to offer up spiritual sacrifices acceptable to God through Jesus Christ.

1 Peter 2:4-5

The steps of a good man are ordered by the Lord, And He delights in his way. Though he fall, he shall not be utterly cast down; For the Lord upholds him with His hand.

Psalm 37:23-24

If anyone is in Christ, he is a new creation; old things have passed away; behold, all things have become new.

2 Corinthians 5:17

These things I have spoken to you, that in Me you may have peace. In the world you will have tribulations; but be of good cheer, I have overcome the world.

John 16:33

My flesh and my heart fail; But God is the strength of my heart and my portion forever.

Psalm 73:26

If any of you lacks wisdom, let him ask of God, who gives to all liberally and without reproach, and it will be given to him.

James 1:5

The Lord is my light and my salvation; Whom shall I fear? The Lord is the strength of my life; Of whom shall I be afraid?

Psalm 27:1

Peace I leave with you, My peace I give to you; not as the world gives do I give to you. Let not your heart be troubled, neither let it be afraid."

John 14:27

Become complete. Be of good comfort, be of one mind, live in peace; and the God of love and peace will be with you.

2 Corinthians 13:11

Be anxious for nothing, but in everything by prayer and supplication, with thanksgiving, let your requests be made known to God; and the peace of God, which surpasses all understanding, will guard your hearts and minds through Christ Jesus.

Philippians 4:6–7

When you pass through the waters, I will be with you; and through the rivers, they shall not overflow you. When you walk through the fire, you shall not be burned, nor shall the flame scorch you.

Isaiah 43:2

Ask of Me, and I will give You the nations for Your inheritance, and the ends of the earth for Your possession.

Psalm 2:8

Those who are wise shall shine like the brightness of the firmament, and those who turn many to righteousness like the stars forever and ever.

Daniel 12:3

But you were washed, but you were sanctified, but you were justified in the name of the Lord Jesus and by the Spirit of our God.

1 Corinthians 6:11

Who may ascend into the hill of the Lord? Or who may stand in His holy place? He who has clean hands and a pure heart, who has not lifted up his soul to an idol, nor sworn deceitfully.

Psalm 24:3-4

But the Lord is faithful, who will establish you and guard you from the evil one.

2 Thessalonians 3:3

For God is not unjust to forget your work and labor of love which you have shown toward His name, in that you have ministered to the saints, and do minister.

Hebrews 6:10

The angel of the Lord encamps all around those who fear Him, and delivers them.

Psalm 34:7

Then those who feared the Lord spoke to one another, and the Lord listened and heard them; so a book of remembrance was written before Him for those who fear the Lord and who meditate on His name.

Malachi 3:16

Yet I will rejoice in the Lord, I will joy in the God of my salvation.

Habakkuk 3:18

For as by one man's disobedience many were made sinners, so also by one Man's obedience many will be made righteous.

Romans 5:19

But know that the Lord has set apart for Himself him who is godly; the Lord will hear when I call to Him.

Psalm 4:3

Chapter 5

I
Am
Enabled
By
God

He gives power to the weak, And to those who have no might He increases strength. Even the youths shall faint and be weary, And the young men shall utterly fall, But those who wait on the Lord Shall renew their strength; They shall mount up with wings like eagles, They shall run and not be weary, They shall walk and not faint.

Isaiah 40:29–31

For whatever is born of God overcomes the world. And this is the victory that has overcome the world—our faith. Who is he who overcomes the world, but he who believes that Jesus is the Son of God?

1 John 5:4-5

Counsel is mine, and sound wisdom; I am understanding, I have strength."

Proverbs 8:14

Direct my steps by Your word, And let no iniquity have dominion over me.

Psalm 119:133

If you abide in Me, and My words abide in you, you will ask what you desire, and it shall be done for you . . . These things I have spoken to you, that My joy may remain in you, and that your joy may be full."

John 15:7,11

Do not be afraid of sudden terror, Nor of trouble from the wicked when it comes; For the Lord will be your confidence, And will keep your foot from being caught.

Proverbs 3:25-26

For God has not given us a spirit of fear, but of power and of love and of a sound mind.

2 Timothy 1:7

Finally, my brethren, be strong in the Lord and in the power of His might.

Ephesians 6:10

Strengthen the weak hands, and make firm the feeble knees. Say to those who are fearful-hearted, "Be strong, do not fear! Behold your God will come with vengeance, with the recompense of God; He will come and save you."

Isaiah 35:3-4

For thus says the Lord God, the Holy One of Israel: "In returning and rest you shall be saved; In quietness and confidence shall be your strength."

Isaiah 30:15

You are of God, little children, and have overcome them, because He who is in you is greater than he who is in the world.

1 John 4:4

Trust in the Lord with all your heart, And lean not to your own understanding; In all your ways acknowledge Him, And He shall direct your paths.

Proverbs 3:5-6

Be of good courage, And He shall strengthen your heart, All you who hope in the Lord.

Psalm 31:24

Therefore do not cast away your confidence, which has great reward. For you have need of endurance, so that after you have done the will of God, you may receive the promise.

Hebrews 10:35-36

For the Lord give wisdom; From His mouth come knowledge and understanding.

Proverbs 2:6

Seek good and not evil, that you may live; so the Lord God of hosts will be with you, as you have spoken.

Amos 5:14

He who overcomes shall be clothed in white garments, and I will not blot out his name from the Book of Life; but I will confess his name before My Father and before His angels."

Revelation 3:5

But now in Christ Jesus you who once were far off have been made near by the blood of Christ. For He Himself is our peace, who has made both one, and has broken down the middle wall of division between us.

Ephesians 2:13–14

For "whoever calls upon the name of the Lord shall be saved."

Romans 10:13

And God is able to make all grace abound toward you, that you, always having all sufficiency in all things, have an abundance for every good work.

2 Corinthians 9:8

I will instruct you and teach you in the way you should go; I will guide you with My eye.

Psalm 32:8

I will bring the blind by a way they did not know; I will lead them in paths they have not known. I will make darkness light before them, and crooked places straight. These things I will do for them, and not forsake them.

Isaiah 42:16

My soul melts from heaviness; Strengthen me according to Your word.

Psalm 119:28

For if these things are yours and abound, you will be neither barren nor unfruitful in the knowledge of our Lord Jesus Christ.

2 Peter 1:8

The Lord God is my strength; He will make my feet like deer's feet, and He will make me walk on my high hills.

Habakkuk 3:19

Ask, and it will be given to you; seek, and you will find; knock, and it will be opened to you. For everyone who asks receives, and he who seeks finds, and to him who knocks it will be opened.

Matthew 7:7-8

I can do all things through Christ who strengthens me.

Philippians 4:13

But thanks be to God, who gives us the victory through our Lord Jesus Christ.

1 Corinthians 15:57

For the Lord God will help Me; therefore I will not be disgraced; therefore I have set My face like a flint, and I know that I will not be ashamed."

Isaiah 50:7